con✓ivio

present

Pelleas and Melisande

by

Maurice Maeterlinck

translated from the French by

Timberlake Wertenbaker

ff

con✓ivio

Convivio is a young company; our first production was *A Night with Constantine Cavafy*, which opened at the King's Head Theatre, Islington, in April 1997. This was devised from the poetry of C.P. Cavafy, music, Greek food and drink, and was the first collaboration between director, Alex Chisholm, and musical directors, Graham Pointer and Nadine Owen. After sell-out performances at the King's Head, the production was successfully revived at other London venues. The production was sponsored by Alpha Bank London.

Other work includes education projects with young people and *Polyphony, Pelleas and Melisande*, an experiment in music, sound and text as part of the BAC's *Sharp Intake of Music* season, 1998.

Future plans for the company include a collaborative production of *Zog* by Peer Wittenbols of Toneelgroep De Federatie in the Netherlands, at Theseum, Theatre for the Arts, in Greece.

Convivio is defined by its method of working: artists work collaboratively in order to develop their art and themselves. Our aim is to bring different artists and audiences together in *a feast of experience*, making new connections and enabling creation.

To find out more about Convivio and our work contact us at:

The Barn, Batchworth Hill House, London Road, Rickmansworth, WD3 1JS

Tel/fax: 01923 72 15 98
E-mail: convivio@compuserve.com

Director's Introduction

It is just over one hundred years since *Pelleas and Melisande*, 'a tragic romance in five acts', was first performed in English. It ran for nine matinees only at the Prince of Wales Theatre with star of the London stage, Mrs Patrick Campbell, in the role of Melisande.

Since then there have been a bare handful of English productions, despite the play's reputation as one of the great classics of European theatre and its popularity in the form of Debussy's opera.

Convivio is therefore delighted to present Maeterlinck's *Pelleas and Melisande* in a new translation by Timberlake Wertenbaker. The translation was broadcast on BBC Radio ten years ago and Timberlake Wertenbaker has since reworked it for the stage. We hope that this performance and publication will revive the fortunes of this fascinating and long-overlooked play.

Alex Chisholm

This programme/playscript went to press while the play was still in rehearsal and the text in performance may differ in some respects from that printed here.

Maurice Maeterlinck

Born in Ghent, Belgium, in 1862, Maurice Polydore Marie Bernard Maeterlinck turned to literature at a young age. In 1889 he published his first collection of poems and a play, *La Princess Maleine.* This already demonstrated his interest in themes of love, death and sacrifice, treated in stylised and poetic language, which came to characterise the symbolist movement in theatre. First performed in 1893, *Pelleas and Melisande* inaugurated the symbolist Théâtre de l'Oeuvre and became recognised as the masterpiece of symbolist drama. Through this and his other works, including *L'Intruse, Les Aveugles* and *L'Oiseau bleu,* Maeterlinck influenced a generation of great theatrical figures: Stanislavsky, Meyerhold, Artaud, Gordon Craig.

In 1911 Maeterlinck was awarded the Nobel Prize for Literature for his work as a playwright, poet and essayist. He died in 1949 in Orlamonde, in France. His influence is still felt on theatre today, with landmark productions of Debussy's opera of *Pelleas and Melisande* by Peter Sellers and Robert Wilson.

Timberlake Wertenbaker

Timberlake Wertenbaker's plays include *New Anatomies* (ICA, London, 1982), *Abel's Sister* (Royal Court, Theatre Upstairs, London, 1984), *The Grace of Mary Traverse* (Royal Court, main stage, London), *Our Country's Good* (Royal Court, main stage, London and Broadway), winner of the Laurence Olivier Play of the Year Award in 1988 and New York Drama Critics' Circle Award for Best New Foreign Play in 1991, *The Love* of *the Nightingale* (Royal Shakespeare Company's Other Place, Stratford-upon-Avon), which won the 1989 Eileen Anderson Central TV Drama Award, *Three Birds Alighting on a Field* (Royal Court, main stage, London), which won the Susan Smith Blackburn Award, Writers' Guild Award and London Critics' Circle Award in 1992, *The Break of Day* (Out of Joint Production, Royal Court, London, and touring, 1995) and *After Darwin* (Hampstead Theatre, London, 1998). She has written the screenplay *of The Children,* based on Edith Wharton's novel, and a BBC2 film entitled *Do Not Disturb.* Translations include Marivaux's *False Admissions* and *Successful Strategies* for Shared Experience, Marivaux's *La Dispute,* Jean Anouilh's *Leocadia,* Maurice Maeterlinck's *Pelleas and Melisande* for BBC Radio, Ariane Mnouchkine's *Mephisto,* adapted for the RSC in 1986, Sophocles' *The Theban Plays* (RSC, London and Stratford, 1991), Euripides' *Hecuba* (San Francisco, 1995), Eduardo de Filippo's *Filumena* (Peter Hall's Company at Piccadilly, 1998), and Pirandello's *Com tu mi vuoi.*

This production of *Pelleas and Melisande* opened at Melbourn Village College, South Cambridgeshire, on 10 March 1999 and then performed at the following venues:

Maltings Arts Centre, St. Albans	12 March
Lion and Unicorn, Gaisford Street, Kentish Town	16–27 March
Cambridge Drama Centre	6–17 April
Pulloxhill Church Hall, Beds	22 April
BAC, Lavender Hill, Battersea	11–15 May

Melbourn Arts Development Group was financially assisted by South Cambridgeshire District Council in bringing *Pelleas and Melisande* to Melbourn.

Many thanks to

Timberlake Wertenbaker and Mel Kenyon at
Casarotto Ramsay, Bill Alexander and the Birmingham Rep,
Cathy Buggenhout and the Belgian Embassy, Tony Seaton
and Melbourn Village College, David Jubb at the
Lion and Unicorn, Ross Brown, Pat Hartley, Noel Gibson
at the Welsh Chapel, the Chisholm family, Lyn Hilton,
Chris Pickles, Peader Kirk and Angela Ballard

GRIFFITHS HICKS
Chartered Accountants

Telephone: 01442 870277

The White House
Lower Kings Road
Berkhampstead
Hertforshire
HP4 2AA

present

PELLEAS AND MELISANDE

by Maurice Maeterlinck
translated by Timberlake Wertenbaker

Characters *in order of speaking*

Servant Woman	Kate Portal
Golaud	Francisco Orjales-Mourente
Melisande	Emily Machon
Genevieve	Lindsay Richardson
Arkel	Andrew Hodgson
Pelleas	Nick Danan
Yniold	Kate Portal
Doctor	Lindsay Richardson

Director	Alex Chisholm
Designer	Rosie Alabaster
Musical Director/Composer	Graham Pointer
Musical Director/Sound Designer	Nadine Owen
Lighting Designer	Alex Chisholm
Wardrobe	Amy Holloway
Assistant Director	Miranda Lundskaer-Neilsen
Puppetry Consultant	Chris Langdon
Poster Photographer	Lindsay Richardson
Press Officer	Maria Balermpa

Company Biographies

Rosie Alabaster – Designer

Trained in theatre design at St. Martins Art College, graduating in 1998. She went straight to Ipswich to design *The Miser* for Andrew Manley at the Wolsey Theatre. *Pelleas and Melisande* is her second professional production.

Alex Chisholm – Director

Trained in directing at Drama Studio London. Founded Convivio and directed *A Night with Constantine Cavafy*. She has directed over 15 productions, including Euripides, Shakespeare, Chekhov, devised and new writing. As an assistant director, work includes Paines Plough, Red Shift, Royal National Theatre and most recently, assisting Bill Alexander at Birmingham Rep on Fay Weldon's *The Four Alice Bakers*.

Nick Danan – Pelleas

Studied English at Oxford and then trained at the Guildford School of Acting. His theatre credits include: *A Grand Wee Game* (Bridewell Theatre), *Briefs* (Lyric Hammersmith Studio), *Gym & Tonic* (Hull Truck), *Poor Ted* (Stopgap) and *Juno and the Paycock* (Leicester Haymarket). He has also appeared in *The Authentick and Ironical History of Henry V* (BBC/OU) and a music video for The Wiseguys.

Andrew Hodgson – Arkel

Acting roles include Andrew Aguecheek in *Twelfth Night*, Squire Sullen in *The Beaux's Stratagem* and Private Boggis in *The Accrington Pals*. He has given a number of song recitals and appeared in the first production of a new opera *The Ansaphone* at the Edinburgh Fringe

Amy Holloway – Wardrobe

Graduated from St. Martin's Theatre Design course in 1998, and has since worked on series of short films and a promenade performance with young people. She has also made models for theatre, TV and museum exhibitions.

Chris Langdon – Puppetry

Trained in animation and film before becoming involved in puppetry. He has subsequently enjoyed working as a sound designer, lighting designer and composer for theatre, often across these disciplines.

Emily Machon – Melisande

Graduated from Drama Studio London last June. TV: Julie Craven in *The Bill*. Theatre: Lucy in *Pale Horse*, Polly in *The Boy Friend*, Vivie in *Mrs Warren's Profession*, Millament in *The Way of the World*, Puck in *A Midsummer Night's Dream*, Frances in *Racing Demons*, Anya in *The Cherry Orchard*.

Francisco Orjales-Mourente – Golaud

Studied at the Laban Centre and Rambert School, London. He has worked for

Threshold Theatre Company at the Edinburgh Fringe, English National Opera and with Pina Bauch, Tanz-theater, Wuppertal. He has also performed in several small-scale choreographic works and is currently training as a Pilates teacher at the Alan Herdman Studios, London.

Nadine Owen – Musical Director

One of the founding members of the sound collective, FP Sound, her previous works include *A Night with Constantine Cavafy, All by Myself* (Quicksilver TC) and the feature film *Guru in Seven*. Currently working on the feature film *Life Cycle* as well as Quicksilver's new show *The Sound Collector.* You can e-mail Nadine on nadineowen@hotmail.com or for details of FP Sound go to http://www.theatresound. demon.co.uk

Graham Pointer – Musical Director

An accomplished musician and composer. Previously played for Ottis Redding JR,

Fergal Sharkey and Eddie Floyd to name but a few. Previous composition work includes *A Night with Constantine Cavafy*, *Weddings of Blood*, West Sussex Youth Theatre and the feature film *Guru in Seven*. Currently lecturing for various institutes and working as a producer.

Kate Portal –
Servant Woman, Yniold

Performed in Convivio's *Polyphony*, *Pelleas and Melisande*. Toured with Graeae Theatre Co. in *Hound* by Maria Oshodi, played Polly Peachum in *The Beggar's Opera* with Path Productions at the Cochrane Theatre. She has worked, mainly as a musician, with Amici Dance Company and Chilian Puppetry Company Teatro Travesura. Kate plays folk fiddle, recently joining a band, Flexible Friends, and runs workshops in music and storytelling.

Lindsay Richardson –
Genevieve, Doctor

Studied at Trinity College of Music after time spent as an art and design lecturer. Studies privately with Hazel Wood. Operatic roles include Alice Flint in the premiere of Diane Burrell's *The Albatross*; Commere in *Four Saints in Three Acts* by, Virgil Thompson; Jack's Mother in Sondheim's *Into the Woods*; and Sorceress in Purcell's *Dido and Aeneas*. Solo work includes Haydn's *Stabat Mater* and Wagner's *Wesendonk* lieder, both at St. John's, Smith Square.

MAURICE MAETERLINCK

Pelleas and Melisande

translated by
Timberlake Wertenbaker

faber and faber

First published in 1999
by Faber and Faber Limited
3 Queen Square, London WC1N 3AU

Typeset by Country Setting, Kingsdown, Kent CT14 8ES
Printed in England by Intype London Ltd

All rights reserved

© Timberlake Wertenbaker, 1999

Timberlake Wertenbaker is hereby identified as author
of this work in accordance with Section 77 of the
Copyright, Designs and Patents Act 1988

All rights whatsoever in this work are strictly reserved.
Applications for permission for any use whatsoever
including performance rights must be made in advance,
prior to any such proposed use, to Casarotto Ramsay Ltd,
National House, 60–66 Wardour Street, London W1V 4ND.
No performance may be given unless a licence has first been obtained.

*This book is sold subject to the condition that it shall not,
by way of trade or otherwise, be lent, resold, hired out
or otherwise circulated without the publisher's prior consent
in any form of binding or cover other than that in which it is
published and without a similar condition including
this condition being imposed on the subsequent purchaser*

A CIP record for this book
is available from the British Library

ISBN 0–571–20201–2

2 4 6 8 10 9 7 5 3 1

Characters

Melisande

Golaud

Pelleas

Yniold

Arkel

Genevieve

Serving Woman

Shepherd

Doctor

Act One

SCENE ONE

The castle door.

Serving Woman I can't open the door.

This door is never opened. Listen to the grating of locks, screech of bolts . . .

It's beginning. The door's opening. Listen to its rasp. It will wake the whole castle.

I've come to wash the threshold . . . there are to be great celebrations, events . . . I'll wash the threshold, the doorway, the doorstep. It's opening wide.

And already so light. The sun rises high over the sea. I'll never get this clean. I need water, more water, but not even the waters of the Great Flood would help me get to the end of it.

SCENE TWO

The forest.
Melisande next to a fountain. Golaud comes on.

Golaud I'll never find my way out of this forest. Traces of blood here . . . I was sure I had wounded it, but now I've lost the beast again. I may have lost myself as well, my dogs don't know where I am . . .

I hear crying. A little girl . . . crying by the fountain! (*He coughs.*) She can't hear me.

He approaches and touches Melisande.

Why are you crying?

Melisande gets up and is about to run away.

5

Golaud Don't be frightened. Why are you crying here all by yourself?

Melisande Don't touch me!

Golaud Please don't be afraid. I wouldn't hurt –
   How beautiful you are!

Melisande If you touch me I'll jump into that water!

Golaud I won't touch you then. I'll stay right here, next to this tree. Has someone hurt you?

Melisande Yes!

   She begins to sob.

Golaud Who is it who has hurt you so?

Melisande They all have!

Golaud And how have they hurt you?

Melisande I can't tell you, I don't want to.

Golaud Come now, you mustn't cry like that. Where have you come from?

Melisande I ran away . . .

Golaud Yes, but where have you run away from?

Melisande And now I'm lost. I don't belong here. And I wasn't born there either . . .

Golaud Where were you born?

Melisande Oh, far away from here . . . very far away . . .

Golaud Look, there's something sparkling down there in the water.

Melisande It's the crown he gave me. It fell into the water when I was crying.

Golaud A crown! Who gave you such a crown? Let me try to retrieve it.

Melisande I don't want it any more. I'd rather die right now, right here, than have that crown.

Golaud The water isn't very deep, I could easily reach it.

Melisande I don't want it. If you bring that crown out of the water, I'll jump in its place.

Golaud Let's leave it there then. It's a very beautiful crown. Has it been a long time since you ran away?

Melisande Yes . . .
   Who are you?

Golaud My name is Golaud. Prince Golaud. I am the grandson of Arkel, King of Allemonde.

Melisande You're already going grey . . .

Golaud Only here, just a little, at the temples.

Melisande What about your beard? It's going grey as well. Why are you looking at me like that?

Golaud I've been looking at your eyes . . . don't you ever close your eyes?

Melisande I close my eyes when it's night-time.

Golaud Why are you looking so surprised?

Melisande You look like a giant.

Golaud I'm only a man, like any other man . . .

Melisande Why did you come here?

Golaud I'm not sure . . . I was hunting a wild boar in the forest. I seem to have taken a wrong turn some-where. You look so young. How old are you?

Melisande I'm beginning to feel cold.

Golaud Would you like to come with me?

Melisande No, I want to stay here.

Golaud You can't stay here all alone all through the night. What is your name?

Melisande My name is Melisande . . .

Golaud You must not stay here, Melisande, come with me.

Melisande I'm staying here.

Golaud You'll be very frightened all by yourself, through the night. No, it's not possible. Come, Melisande, give me your hand.

Melisande Don't touch me!

Golaud Don't shout. I shan't touch you any more, but you must come with me. The night will be very black, very cold. Come with me . . .

Melisande Where?

Golaud I don't know. I seem to be lost as well.

SCENE THREE

A room in the castle.
  Genevieve, Arkel.

Genevieve This is what he's written to his brother. 'Pelleas, I found her one evening, sobbing in the forest where I had lost my way. I don't know how old she is, who she is, where she comes from and I don't dare ask her. She must have been terrorised and when you ask her what happened to her, she bursts into tears like a child and then she cries so bitterly, you fear for her life. When I found her, she was wearing the clothes of a princess, but they had been shredded by brambles. A golden

8

crown had fallen from her head. It's now six months
since I married her and I know no more about her than
on the day I first met her.

'Pelleas, my dear Pelleas, whom I love more than a
brother even if we do not share the same father, can you
prepare them for my return? I know that my mother will
forgive me, but I am afraid of the king, our venerable
grandfather, I am afraid of Arkel, despite his kindness.
I know that I will have upset all of his political plans
with this marriage. Nor may a man as wise as he find
in Melisande's translucent beauty an excuse for my mad-
ness. If, however, he is willing to receive her as he would
receive his own daughter, then three days after you receive
this letter shine a light from the tower that overlooks the
sea. I will look for it from the ship and if I do not see it,
then I will go on, I will sail on and never come back.'

What do you say to this?

Arkel I have nothing to say about it. He probably acted
as he had to. I am an old man, I cannot even see into my
own self, how can I judge the actions of others? One
must close one's eyes, to forgive, or at the very least to
see better into one's own self. His actions seem strange
to us, no more. He is no longer a young man and yet,
like a youth, he marries a little girl he finds by chance
next to a fountain in the forest. It seems strange to us
because we can't see the shape of a destiny, even if it's
our own. I thought to make him happy with this
marriage to Princess Ursula. He'd been so lonely since
his wife's death. And yes, this marriage would have ended
a long war, ancient hatreds. In the end, he did not wish
it and it must be as he wished. He knows his own future
better than I do and I would never willingly block
someone's fate. Perhaps there is a reason for all this . . .

Genevieve But he has always been so cautious, so serious.
I would have understood if Pelleas had done such a

thing, but Golaud, and at his age. Since his wife's death, he's lived only for his little son, Yniold. He only agreed to remarry because you wanted him to. And suddenly – and who is he bringing to us? A little girl picked up on his wanderings. He meets her in the middle of a forest and he forgets everything. What are we to do?

Arkel Who's there?

Genevieve Pelleas. He's been crying.

Arkel Is that you, Pelleas? Come into the light so that I can see you.

Pelleas Grandfather, there was another letter with my brother's. It's from Marcellus and he tells me that he's about to die and that he wants to see me.

Arkel Would you leave before your own brother returns, Pelleas? Marcellus may not be as ill as he believes.

Pelleas You can read death in every line of his letter. He says he knows the day he will die and that if I want to get to him in time I mustn't delay. If I wait for Golaud I could be too late . . .

Arkel Wait a little. We don't know what will happen here when Golaud returns. And there is your father, lying in the room above us, who may be even more ill than your friend . . . How are you to choose between a father and a friend?

Genevieve Have the light shine from the window tonight, Pelleas.

SCENE FOUR

Outside, in front of the castle.
Genevieve and Melisande come on.

Melisande It's so dark in these gardens. And this thick forest . . . enclosing the castle . . .

Genevieve Yes, Melisande, I was surprised as well when I first came here. Everyone is surprised. There are places the sun never reaches. And yet, one becomes accustomed to it, quite quickly. It's been nearly forty years since I first came here . . . Look towards the other side, and you'll have the light from the sea.

Melisande I hear a noise somewhere below us.

Genevieve Someone is climbing towards us. It's Pelleas. He still seems exhausted, he waited for you for such a long time . . .

Melisande He hasn't seen us yet.

Genevieve I think he has seen us, but he doesn't know what to do about it . . . Pelleas, is that you?

Pelleas comes on.

Pelleas Yes . . . I wanted to look at the sea.

Genevieve So did we. We were searching for a little brightness. Here, there is a little more light than else-where.
And yet, look how black the sea has turned.

Pelleas We'll have a storm tonight. We often have them. And yet the sea is so still at the moment . . . you could sail away without noticing and never return.

Melisande Something is moving out of the harbour.

11

Pelleas It must be a large ship . . . look how high her lights are, we'll see her later when she sails into that strip of brightness over there.

Genevieve We may not be able to see her, there's a thick fog blanketing the sea . . .

Pelleas The fog seems to be lifting, slowly . . .

Melisande I can see a tiny light I never saw before, there, over there . . .

Pelleas It's a lighthouse. There are many others we haven't yet been able to see.

Melisande The ship has moved into the light . . . she's already so far away . . .

Pelleas It's a foreign ship. She's much bigger than any of ours.

Melisande It's the ship that brought me here. I recognise the large sails.

Pelleas The sea will be very rough tonight . . .

Melisande Why is she sailing away? . . . I can hardly see the ship any more . . . what if she is wrecked on the rocks, what if she sinks?

Pelleas The night comes down so fast.

A silence.

Genevieve No one is speaking? Don't you two have anything more to say each other? . . . it's time to go back into the castle. Show Melisande the way, Pelleas, I want to go and see Yniold for a moment.

Genevieve leaves.

Pelleas There's nothing more to be seen on the water now, the sea lies empty.

Melisande I can see more lights . . .

Pelleas Those are from the other lighthouses . . . Can you hear that? It's the wind rising from the sea . . . Let's go down this way. Will you give me your hand?

Melisande Look! My hands are full of flowers and leaves.

Pelleas Let me hold you by the arm then, the path is steep and rough and it's very dark . . . I may go away tomorrow . . .

Melisande Why? . . . Why are you going away?

Act Two

SCENE ONE

By a fountain in the grounds.
Pelleas, Melisande.

Pelleas Are you wondering where I'm taking you? I often come and sit here at noon, when the gardens have become too hot, but it's stifling today, even under the shade of the trees.

Melisande The water is so clear.

Pelleas And as fresh as a winter's day. This is an old and abandoned fountain. It was believed to work miracles and restore sight to the blind. It is still known as the 'fountain of the blind'.

Melisande But it no longer restores sight?

Pelleas No one comes here any more now that the King himself is almost blind.

Melisande How solitary it feels here . . . you can't even hear a ripple of sound . . .

Pelleas A most unusual silence always hangs over this fountain . . . listen: you can hear the water sleeping. Would you like to sit on the edge of this marble basin? The sun never penetrates the branches of this lime tree.

Melisande I want to lie down on the marble. I want to see all the way down to the bottom of the water.

Pelleas No one's ever seen down to the bottom, the water seems as deep as the sea. It could be rising up from the centre of the earth.

Melisande Perhaps if something were to shine on the bottom, we could see how deep it was.

Pelleas Please don't lean so far over . . .

Melisande But I want to touch the water . . .

Pelleas Be careful, you might slip . . . Let me hold your hand.

Melisande No. I want to plunge both hands into this water . . . my hands don't feel well today.

Pelleas Be careful, Melisande Look at your hair.

Melisande I can't reach down to the water.

Pelleas But your hair plunged deep down into it.

Melisande Ah yes, my hair can reach much further than my hands.

A silence . . .

Pelleas Was it also by a fountain that he found you?

Melisande Yes . . .

Pelleas What did he say to you?

Melisande Nothing. I can't remember.

Pelleas Did he stand very close to you?

Melisande Yes. He wanted to kiss me.

Pelleas And you didn't want him to?

Melisande Look, I saw something down there, at the bottom of the water.

Pelleas Be careful, you'll fall in. What are you playing with?

Melisande I'm playing with the ring he gave me.

Pelleas Be careful, you might lose it.

Melisande I'm sure of my hands.

Pelleas Don't play with it like that. Not over water that is so deep.

Melisande My hands never shake.

Pelleas See how the ring glitters in the sun. You mustn't throw it up so high.

Melisande Oh!

Pelleas It fell in?

Melisande Yes, it fell into the water.

Pelleas Where is it?

Melisande I can't see it going down, I can't see it at all.

Pelleas I think I see it shining . . . down there . . .

Melisande Where?

Pelleas There, down there . . .

Melisande No, that's not it, that's not it at all. It's lost. All that's left on the water now is a widening circle lapping the fountain's edge. What are we going to do now?

Pelleas There's no need to worry so much over a ring. It's nothing, we might find it anyway. If not, we'll find another ring . . .

Melisande We'll never find that ring again and we won't find any other rings either. And yet, I was so sure I was holding it in my hands. I had already closed my hands over the ring, but it fell through my hands . . . I threw it too high, up towards the sun.

Pelleas Come with me now. We'll return here another day and look again. It's time to go. Someone could see us here. I heard the bells strike noon as the ring fell in the water . . .

Melisande What are we going to say to Golaud if he asks about the ring?

Pelleas We must tell Golaud the truth, the whole truth.

SCENE TWO

A room in the castle.
  Golaud lies on a bed, Melisande by his side.

Golaud It's nothing. I still can't understand how it happened. I was out hunting as usual in the forest and suddenly, my horse bolted, for no reason. He must have been startled by something unusual. I was listening to the twelve strokes of noon and on the twelfth stroke he suddenly took fright and galloped like a blinded madman into a tree. And then I heard nothing more. I don't know what happened. I fell down and my horse must have fallen on top of me. I felt as if the forest had fallen on top of my chest, and my heart had been crushed and ground to pieces. But see, my heart is made of sterner stuff and it seems to be nothing at all.

Melisande Would you like to drink a little water?

Golaud No. I'm not thirsty.

Melisande Would you like another pillow under your head? There's a small drop of blood on this one.

Golaud No. It's not worth the trouble. My mouth bled a little while ago, it might start bleeding again.

Melisande Are you sure? Are you in very much pain?

Golaud No. It's not the first time after all. I'm inured to blood and to iron. You needn't worry, the bones I have around my heart are not the brittle bones of a child, they won't break easily.

Melisande Close your eyes, try to sleep, I'll stay by your side through the night.

Golaud No, I don't want you to tire yourself over nothing. I'll sleep like a big baby. What is it, Melisande, why are you crying, now, suddenly?

Melisande (*sobbing*) I'm not well . . . I'm suffering too . . .

Golaud What's wrong with you, Melisande?

Melisande I don't know what it is . . . I feel I must tell you this today, my lord, I must tell you that . . . I am not happy here . . .

Golaud What's happened, Melisande? What is it? Has someone caused you harm? Has someone hurt your feelings?

Melisande No. That's not it . . . but I can't live here any more. I don't know why . . . I want to go away. I know I'll die if I stay here.

Golaud But something must have happened? You must be hiding something from me. Tell me the truth, Melisande. Is it the King? Is it my mother? Is it Pelleas?

Melisande No, no. It isn't Pelleas. It isn't anyone in particular. How could you understand? . . .

Golaud Come now, be more sensible, Melisande. What do you want me to do?
  You're not a child any longer . . . Is it because of me? Am I the one you want to leave?

Melisande No, I would like to leave with you . . . It's just that . . . I can't live here any more.

Golaud There must be a reason for this. Can't you get used to the life we lead here? This castle is very old as

well as very dark . . . It's a cold and cavernous place
and all those who live here are already old. And the
countryside is grim with its circles of forests. But one
could make all this more cheerful with a little effort. And
then, happiness doesn't come to us every day, we must
learn to accept things as they are . . . Tell me what you
want and I'll do anything you ask of me.

Melisande That's what it is. You can never see the light
of the sky. It wasn't until this morning that I saw a clear
sky – for the first time . . .

Golaud And is that all that is making you cry like that,
my poor little Melisande? Come, you're no longer at
an age when such things should make you cry. And
isn't summer coming soon? Then you'll be able to look
up at the sky every day if you want to, and then next
year . . . Come now, give me your hand, give me both
your little hands. (*He taker her hands.*) Oh, those
delicate little hands of yours, I could crush them like
the petals of a flower . . . Melisande? Where is the ring
I gave you?

Melisande The ring?

Golaud Yes, my wedding ring? Where is it?

Melisande I think . . . I think it must have fallen off . . .

Golaud Fallen off? Fallen off where? You haven't lost it,
have you?

Melisande No, it must have fallen off . . . but I think I
know where it is . . .

Golaud Where?

Melisande You know . . . you know . . . the cave by the
sea?

Golaud Yes.

Melisande Well, there, it must have fallen off in there . . . yes, I remember now. I went there this morning to look for some shells for little Yniold . . . there are some very beautiful shells . . . it slipped from my finger . . . and then the sea came in, I must have left the cave without being able to find it.

Golaud Are you sure that's where you lost it?

Melisande Yes, I'm absolutely sure . . . it slipped off, and then suddenly, there was the sound of the waves coming in . . .

Golaud You must go there and search for it immediately.

Melisande Now? In the darkness?

Golaud I would have preferred to have lost everything I own rather than that ring. You don't know anything about it. You don't know where the ring comes from. The tide will be high tonight, the sea could come and take the ring away before you get there. You must hurry. You must go and look for it immediately.

Melisande I'm frightened to go there by myself.

Golaud Find someone to go with you, anyone, but go right now, do you hear me. Hurry. Ask Pelleas to go with you.

Melisande Pelleas? Go with Pelleas? But Pelleas won't want to . . .

Golaud Pelleas will do anything you ask of him.Go now. Hurry. I won't be able to go to sleep until I have the ring.

Melisande I am not happy here . . . !

 She goes out, crying.

SCENE THREE

In front of the cave.
  Pelleas and Melisande come in.

Pelleas (*very agitated*) Here it is. It is so dark it's hard to separate the cave's entrance from the night . . . not even the stars can light up this side. We must wait until the moon rips open a cloud above us and sheds its light on the cave. Then we'll be able to go in without fear. Some parts of the cave are treacherous, the path is narrow and runs between two lakes whose depths have never been fathomed. I didn't think to bring a lamp or a torch but I believe the light from the sky will be enough. Have you ever been inside this cave before?

Melisande No . . .

Pelleas Let's go in now. If he questions you, you'll have to be able to describe the place where you lost the ring.
  This cave is vast and very beautiful. Stalactites in the shapes of plants and people stand sentinel inside and shadows of a blueish hue criss-cross the darkness. They say many treasures have been hidden down here and that you can still see the remnants of ancient shipwrecks. It's said one must never go into the cave without a guide. Some who have come down here have never returned. Even I don't have the courage to go in too far. When you light a lamp and look up at the vault of the cave you can see tiny stars as if this were a magic firmament. They say it comes from sparkling fragments of crystal or salt encrusted in the rock. Look, the sky is opening up now, and freeing the moonlight for us. Give me your hand, you mustn't tremble so, Melisande, there is no danger at all, we'll stop as soon as we have lost the light from the sea . . . Are you frightened by the sounds coming from the cave? It's no more than the rumble of the sea through

the rocks, or perhaps the echo of the silence. The sea is troubled tonight . . . Here comes the light . . .

The moon lights the entrance to the cave and some way inside it. And there, deep inside the cave can be seen three old people with white hair, dressed in rags, sitting one next to the other in a row, holding each other propped up and sleeping against the rock.

Melisande Ah!

Pelleas What is it?

Melisande There's . . . there's . . .

Pelleas Yes, I saw them as well.

Melisande Please, let's go.

Pelleas It's only three old beggars who've fallen asleep against the rock. A famine has gripped this land and lays it to waste, but why have they come here to sleep?

Melisande Let's go. Let's get away.

Pelleas Don't speak too loud, we mustn't wake them up. They're sleeping so soundly . . . come with me.

Melisande No, leave me, leave me alone, I'd rather walk by myself.

Pelleas We'll come back here another day . . .

They go.

SCENE FOUR

Rooms in the castle.
Arkel, Pelleas.

Arkel And so you see, Pelleas, everything militates against such a fruitless journey. We kept hidden from

you until today the real state of your father's health, but
I am afraid there may be no more hope for him. That
ought to be enough to stop you in your tracks. And
then, there are so many other reasons . . .

How can you abandon us at a time when our enemies
are harrying us and our own people are dying of hunger
and murmuring against our rule?

And why do you feel such a need for this journey?
Your friend Marcellus is already dead. Life holds more
serious obligations than a visit to a grave site. You say
you're becoming weary of the enforced idleness of your
life here. Yes, action and duty can be found on the road,
but the one who travels too hastily often misses them.
It is often best to wait for these to come to your own
doorstep and welcome them in when they pass by. And
they do pass by, Pelleas, every day. Have you never
noticed them, beckoning? I may be almost blind, but
I will teach you to see them, when you are ready.

Pelleas, if you really feel that your whole being
demands this journey of you, then I cannot forbid it.
You must know, better than I ever can, what experiences
you require for your life, and only you can sense the
shape of your destiny. All I am asking of you is to wait
a little until we know what is going to happen.

Pelleas How much longer must I wait?

Arkel A few weeks, perhaps only a few days.

Pelleas Very well, I will wait . . .

Act Three

SCENE ONE

Rooms in the castle.
Pelleas and Melisande.
Melisande is spinning with her distaff at the back of the room.

Pelleas Yniold hasn't come back yet.

Melisande He said he heard some noises in the hall.

Pelleas Melisande . . .

Melisande Yes, Pelleas . . .

Pelleas How can you still see well enough to spin?

Melisande I can work in the dark.

Pelleas It feels as if everyone in the castle has gone to sleep. Golaud hasn't returned from the hunt yet. It's getting very late . . . Does his fall still hurt him?

Melisande He says he doesn't feel pain any more.

Pelleas He ought to be more careful. He doesn't have the body of a twenty-year-old any more.
  I can see the crowd of stars through the window and the light of the moon bathing the trees. It's late. He won't come back now.

  A knock on the door.

Who is it? Come in.

  Yniold opens the door and comes into the room.

Was it you knocking in that way, Yniold? That's no way to knock on a door, as if something terrible has just happened.

Yniold I only knocked once, gently.

Pelleas It's getting late. Your Papa won't be back tonight. It's time for you to go to bed now.

Yniold I won't go to bed before you do.

Pelleas What's this? What are you saying?

Yniold I'm saying I won't go before you do . . .

Yniold bursts into tears and goes over to find comfort with Melisande.

Melisande What's the matter, Yniold, why are you crying suddenly?

Yniold (*sobbing*) Because . . . because . . . oh . . .

Melisande Why, Yniold, you must tell me why . . .

Yniold Mama, you're going to go away.

Melisande What's come over you, Yniold? I've never even dreamt of going away from here.

Yniold Yes, you have. And now Papa is gone. Papa isn't coming back and then you're going to go away as well . . . I've seen it.

Melisande There's never even been a question of my going, Yniold, never. What can you have seen to make you think I was going away?

Yniold You said some things to Uncle that I couldn't hear . . .

Pelleas He's half asleep, he's been dreaming . . . Yniold, come and look out of the window. Look at the swans out there, they're fighting with the dogs.

Yniold The dogs are chasing the swans away . . . wings, wings beating . . . beating down the water . . . they're afraid.

Pelleas comes back to Melisande.

Pelleas He's falling asleep. He's fighting against it, but he can't keep his eyes open any longer.

Melisande 'Saint Daniel and Saint Michael,
   Saint Michael and Saint Raphael . . . '

Yniold is still at the window.

Yniold Mama! Mama!

Melisande gets up abruptly.

Melisande What is it, Yniold?

Yniold I saw something move in front of the window.

Pelleas and Melisande run to the window.

Pelleas I can't see anything.

Melisande I can't see anything either . . .

Yniold There, over there . . . but it's not there any more.

Pelleas He doesn't know what he's saying. He saw the moonlight casting strange reflections on the trees. Or perhaps something moved across the road below or moved across his sleep . . . I think he's finally fallen into a deep sleep.

Yniold Papa, it's Papa, I'm going to meet him.

He runs off.
   A silence.

Pelleas They're coming up the stairs . . .

Golaud comes in with Yniold who is holding a small lantern.

Golaud You were waiting in this darkness?

Yniold I brought a big light, Mama.

He lifts up the lantern and looks at Melisande.

You've been crying.

He lifts the lantern up to Pelleas and look at him in turn.

And so have you, Uncle, you've been crying as well. Papa, they've been crying, both of them.

Golaud Yniold, you mustn't shine the light directly into their eyes like that.

SCENE TWO

One of the castle turrets. A walkway goes around it underneath.
Melisande is at the window, combing her very long and unbound hair.

Melisande
Three blind maidens
(Hope against hope)
Three blind maidens
Let down a rope.

Is anyone there
(You and me too)
Is anyone there
Asks the most fair.

It's the King's son
(Hope against hope)
It's the King's son
Says the tall one.

No, sighs the third
(Hope against hope)
No, sighs the third
It's a sea-bird.

Pelleas comes along the walkway.

Pelleas Hello, hello, hello, ho.

Melisande Who is there?

Pelleas Me and me too. What are you doing at that window singing like a bird from a faraway land?

Melisande I'm arranging my hair for the night.

Pelleas Is that what I see streaming down the wall? I thought it was an escaped ray of sunlight lingering into the night . . .

Melisande I opened the window . . . the night seemed so soft.

Pelleas There are innumerable stars tonight, I've never seen so many . . . the moon still shines over the sea . . . don't stay in the shadows like that, Melisande, lean over a little, I want to see your hair when it's down.

Melisande leans over out of the window.

Pelleas Melisande, how beautiful you look . . . lean over more, let me come closer to you.

Melisande I can't lean over any further.

Pelleas And I can't reach any higher. Please let me have your hand tonight . . . let me have your hand before I go away. I'm leaving tomorrow.

Melisande No, don't. No.

Pelleas Yes, I'm going away, I'm leaving tomorrow . . . let me have your hand, let me feel your fragile little hand on my lips . . .

Melisande Not if you're leaving. If you're leaving I won't give you my hand.

Pelleas Please, give me your hand.

Melisande You won't go away then? I can see something in the shadows.

Pelleas Where? No, I can only see the branches of the willow trees drooping over the wall.

Melisande Further down, much further down, over there, in the garden.

Pelleas I'll go and see what it is later, but first I must have your hand.

Melisande Here it is, I can't lean over any further.

Pelleas I can't reach high enough to kiss it.

Melisande I can't lean over any further, I'm about to fall down as it is, oh, my hair, my hair is coming down the tower wall.

Her hair falls over and floods Pelleas.

Pelleas What's this? Your hair climbs down to me, your hair, your golden hair is tumbling down the turret wall. Your hair falls through my hands, nestles in my arms, I can cover your hair with my kisses, I can wrap myself up in your hair, Melisande, a scarf of gold entwines itself around my neck. I won't let it go for the rest of the night, I'll hold your hair tight in my hands.

Melisande Leave me, Pelleas, you're going to make me fall over.

Pelleas I've never seen such hair as yours Melisande, look, it's cascaded from such a height, it's poured down to my heart and drowned it. Your hair is soft and warm like the wings of the angels, your hair is a gift from the heavens and now its radiance makes even the light of paradise seem dull . . . I can't hold onto your hair any more, it's running away from me, escaping down the branches of the willow tree, your trembling, palpitating hair, fluttering in my hands like a flock of golden birds. Ah yes, and your hair loves me, it loves me much more tenderly than you do.

Melisande Leave me alone, Pelleas, someone could come this way.

Pelleas You can't get away. I'll hold you prisoner for the night.

Melisande Pelleas!

Pelleas You'll never get away. And when I kiss your hair, Melisande, it is all of you I'll cover with my kisses. Because it's only in the tongues of fire of your hair that I no longer feel any pain. Can you hear my kisses? They're climbing up a thousand golden threads and each thread holds a thousand of my kisses, and when I'm not there my kisses will still be marching up along their paths of gold to reach you. Look, now I can open my hands, but you can no longer free yourself from me.

Doves fly out of the tower and circle around.

Melisande What's that, Pelleas, there's something flying around me.

Pelleas It's the doves from the tower . . . I must have frightened them and now they're flying away.

Melisande But those are my doves, Pelleas. Please, leave me alone, we must go. What if the doves never came back?

Pelleas Why wouldn't they come back to you?

Melisande They could get lost in the dark. I have to lift up my head, let me go, I can hear footsteps. I think it's Golaud . . . he's heard us.

Pelleas Wait. Your hair has become tangled in the willow branches. It's so dark.

Golaud comes on.

Golaud Pelleas! What are you doing here?

Pelleas What am I doing here? I –

Golaud Don't lean so far out of the window, Melisande, you'll fall. Do you know how late it is? It's almost midnight. You mustn't play like that in the dark. You're both such children!

He laughs nervously

Come with me, Pelleas.

SCENE THREE

The castle vaults.
  Golaud and Pelleas.

Golaud Take care, Pelleas. This way, come this way. Have you never come down to the castle vaults before?

Pelleas Once, a long time ago . . .

Golaud They're immense. It seems to be a series of interpenetrating caves and God knows where they lead in the end. The whole of the castle is built on top of these caves. Can you smell the deadly odour that suffuses this place? I believe it comes from a small and stagnant underground lake which I'll show you in a moment. Take care. Walk in front of me, the light from my lantern will guide your steps. I'll warn you when we come to the lake.

They walk in silence.

Pelleas! Stop!

Golaud seizes Pelleas's arm.

Couldn't you see?
   Another step and you would have fallen into the abyss.

Pelleas I couldn't see. There was no more light from the lantern.

Golaud I tripped over something myself. But if I hadn't held you by the arm . . . Now here is the stagnant water. If we walk to the end of that rock which overhangs it, you can lean over and the smell will hit you in the face.

Pelleas I can smell it from here. It's the odour of the grave.

Golaud Keep going. This is the smell that on some days poisons the air of the castle. The King doesn't believe that it comes from here, but I think we need to fill in this cave. Indeed, it's time to have a look at all of these vaults. Have you noticed the deep cracks slithering like lizards along these walls and the piles of crumbling stone? There is something at work here which no one suspects and one of these days, if we're not careful, the whole castle could sink into the sea. What's to be done? No one is willing to come down here . . . look again at those cracks, zigzagging over the chasm . . . here it is again. The odour of death . . . can you smell it, Pelleas?

Pelleas It's rising all around us.

Golaud Lean over, I'll hold you. No, I won't hold your hand, it could slip, I'll hold you by the arm. Look into the abyss, Pelleas, look.

Pelleas I'm suffocating, it's so hot.

Golaud Careful.

Pelleas It will be hot all afternoon. I saw Melisande and our mother at the window as we came down.

Golaud They must have been looking for some shade. Speaking of Melisande, I heard all that happened and was said last night. I know that it's only children's games you two play, but it must never happen again. Melisande is very young and impressionable. She must be treated with great care, especially as she might be expecting a child. She's so fragile. It's not the first time I've noticed there might be something between the two of you . . . you're older than she is . . . I only need to mention this once . . . Avoid her, but don't be obvious about it . . . look into that darkness.

Pelleas I can't breathe! What's happened to the light?

Pelleas turns to Golaud

Are you all right?

Golaud (*shaking*) I was moving the lantern to examine the damage to the walls . . .

SCENE FOUR

In front of the castle.
  Golaud and Yniold.

Golaud Let's sit here, Yniold. Come on my lap. We can watch what is going on in the forest from here. I haven't seen much of you lately, you're always with Melisande . . . it seems you're abandoning me as well. Look, it so happens we're sitting under her windows. Perhaps she's saying her prayers as we speak. Tell me, Yniold, Melisande spends a lot of time with Uncle Pelleas, doesn't she?

Yniold Yes, Papa. She's with him all the time when you're not there.

Golaud Ah! – And yet, I've been told they don't like each other very much Uncle Pelleas and Melisande . . . is that not so?

Yniold Yes, that's so, Papa.

Golaud Really? I see. What is it they quarrel about?

Yniold The door.

Golaud The door? What are you talking about? Explain all this to me a little more clearly, why do they quarrel about the door?

Yniold It's not supposed to be open.

Golaud Someone doesn't want the door to be open? Is that what they quarrel about?

Yniold I don't know, Papa. The light.

Golaud I'm not talking about the light. We'll talk about the light later on. I'm talking about the door. Answer. It's about time you learned to make some sense. Don't keep putting your hand in your mouth like that!

Yniold I won't do it again, ever.

Yniold begins to cry.

Golaud Why are you crying? What happened?

Yniold You hurt me, Papa.

Golaud I hurt you? Where? I must have hurt you without knowing it.

Yniold Here, on my arm, you hurt my arm.

Golaud I didn't mean to hurt you. Come now, Yniold, don't cry any more. I'll give you a present tomorrow.

Yniold A present? What kind of present?

Golaud A bow and some arrows. Now tell me what you know about the door.

Yniold Big arrows?

Golaud Yes, yes, very big arrows. But tell me why they don't want the door to be left opened. Come now, will you answer me! No, stop it, don't start crying again. I'm not angry with you. We're going to talk very quietly just like Melisande and Uncle Pelleas. What do they talk about when they're together?

Yniold Pelleas and Mama?

Golaud Yes, what do they talk about?

Yniold They talk about me. They always talk about me.

Golaud And what do they say about you?

Yniold They say I'll grow to be very tall one day.

Golaud Ah, misery, I'm like a blind man searching for a treasure at the bottom of the ocean – and all of you – no, now listen to me, Yniold, I wasn't paying attention before, but now we're going to talk properly. Don't Uncle Pelleas and Mama ever talk about me when I'm not there?

Yniold Yes, Papa, they're always talking about you.

Golaud Ha! And what do they say about me?

Yniold They say one day I'll grow to be as tall as you.

Golaud Do you always stay close to them?

Yniold Yes. Always, Papa.

Golaud Don't they ever tell you to go and play somewhere else?

Yniold No, Papa. They become frightened when I'm not there.

Golaud Frightened? How do you know they're frightened?

Yniold Because Mama always tell me to stay close to her. And they're unhappy but they keep laughing.

Golaud That doesn't mean they're afraid . . .

Yniold Yes, Papa, I know Mama is frightened. They're always crying in the darkness.

Golaud Crying!

Yniold And she's always so pale, Papa.

Golaud Oh my god, give me patience!

Yniold What is it, Papa?

Golaud Nothing, Yniold, I thought I saw a wolf in the forest. But anyway, they get on well, don't they? I'm very happy to hear they like each other. Do they kiss each other sometimes?

Yniold Kiss each other? No Papa, never. Well, yes, once, once when it was raining hard.

Golaud They kissed each other, did they? How did they kiss each other?

Yniold gives Golaud a kiss on the mouth, laughing.

Yniold Like this, Papa. Your beard tickles. And it's going grey all over.

The window under which they are sitting lights up suddenly and the light falls on them.

It's Mama, she's lit her lamp.

Golaud Yes, now we can see.

Yniold Let's go in, Papa.

Golaud No, child, let's stay in the shadows a little longer. There are so many things we still don't know . . . Do you see those poor people who are trying to light a fire in the forest, but they can't because it's too wet?

And look at the gardener over there trying to lift a tree that fell across the path, but it's too heavy for him . . . there's nothing to be done about all that . . .

Would you like to see Mama?

Yniold Oh yes, Papa, I always want to see her.

Golaud I'm going to lift you up to the window. It's too high for me . . .

Golaud lifts up Yniold.

Don't make any noise. It would frighten Mama. Can you see her? Is she in her room?

Yniold Yes and there's so much light.

Golaud Is she alone?

Yniold No. Uncle Pelleas is there as well.

Golaud Him! –

Yniold You're hurting me, Papa!

Golaud I slipped, I won't hurt you any more. Now speak softly. Look. What are they doing?

Yniold They're not doing anything. They're waiting for something.

Golaud Are they very close to each other?

Yniold No, Papa.

Golaud What about the bed? Are they close to the bed?

Yniold The bed? I can't see the bed.

Golaud Speak more quietly, they could hear you. Are they talking to each other?

Yniold No, Papa, they're not talking to each other.

Golaud What are they doing then! They must be doing something!

Yniold They're looking at the light.

Golaud Both of them?

Yniold Yes.

Golaud And they're not saying anything?

Yniold No, Papa, and they're not closing their eyes at all.

Golaud Aren't they moving closer to each other?

Yniold No, they're not moving at all.
    They're both standing against the wall.

Golaud Are they making gestures, some signs to each other? Are they looking at each other?

Yniold No, papa, and they never close their eyes either. I'm frightened.

Golaud Quiet! Are they moving now?

Yniold No, please put me down, I'm frightened.

Golaud What can you be frightened of? Keep looking!

Yniold I don't want to look any more, Papa, I don't want to see anything else. Put me down!

Golaud Keep looking!

Yniold I'm going to scream. Put me down! Please! Put me down!

Golaud Come, let's go and see what's happened.

Act Four

SCENE ONE

A hallway in the castle.
  Pelleas and Melisande come in separately and meet.

Pelleas Can I see you tonight? I have to speak to you.

Melisande Yes.

Pelleas I've just come from my father's room. The doctor says he's saved, and yet this morning I had this terrible premonition that today would end in disaster. They've opened all the windows in my father's room. He's talking, he seems happy. He even recognised me. He took my hand and said with that strange expression he's had since he's been ill: 'Is that you, Pelleas? I had never noticed before that you have the solemn and friendly face of someone who won't live very long.' He told me I must travel. I'm going to do as he says. I can hear people behind this door, tell me quickly, will I see you tonight?

Melisande Where do you want me to come?

Pelleas Come to the fountain of the blind. Will you?

Melisande Yes.

Pelleas It will be our last evening. I'm going to travel. You won't see me any more.

Melisande Don't say that, Pelleas, I'll always see you, I'll always look at you . . .

Pelleas You'll look, but I'll be far away. I'm full of happiness and yet the whole weight of earth and sky seems to be crushing me.

39

Melisande What's happened, Pelleas, I can't understand you.

Pelleas I can hear people talking behind this door. Some travellers came to the castle this morning . . .

They go out separately.

SCENE TWO

Rooms in the castle (or: same as before).
Arkel and Melisande

Arkel At last, Melisande, Illness has fled from this house with her dread companion Death. A small ray of sunshine is penetrating the castle walls. I'm afraid we've done nothing since your arrival but whisper behind closed doors. I felt so sorry for you: you came to us full of joy, like a child looking forward to a party but, the moment you walked into the Great Hall, I saw your face cloud over. And perhaps your soul as well. You seemed so lost, like someone standing in the middle of a beautiful and sunny meadow waiting for a disaster to strike.

You're much too young and beautiful to live night and day under the shadowy exhalations of death. All that will change now. I've learned to believe in the logic of events and I've observed that young and beautiful beings create around them events that are also young, beautiful and happy. You'll be the one to open the door to a new era. Come to me, child, why are you standing there without a word for me, without even raising your eyes? I only kissed you once on the day you arrived and yet old men need to feel on their lips the soft touch of a woman's forehead or the silkiness of a child's cheek – to keep death at bay for a little while longer. Are you frightened of my old lips? Ah, Melisande, I've felt such pity for you!

40

Melisande I wasn't unhappy, Grandfather.

Arkel You may be one of those people who are unhappy without knowing it.

Golaud comes in.

Golaud Pelleas is leaving tonight.

Arkel There's blood on your forehead, what's happened to you?

Golaud Nothing. Brambles.

Melisande Lower your head a little, my lord and I'll wipe your forehead.

Golaud Don't touch me! I have nothing to say to you. I came looking for my sword.

Melisande It's here, on the prie-Dieu.

Golaud Bring it to me. (*to Arkel*) They've found another peasant who's died of starvation on the beach. It seems they all want to come here and stamp their death on our eyes. Well, Melisande? My sword? Why are you shaking so? I'm not going to kill you, I only want to test the blade. And why are you looking at me with the pity one throws down at a beggar? I'm not asking you for alms. Do you think you'll find something in my eyes without letting me ever find anything in yours? Have you seen those eyes, Grandfather, how big they are, how proud and pure? What do you see in those eyes, Grandfather?

Arkel Only great innocence.

Golaud A great innocence, oh yes, they're beyond innocence, they're more limpid than the eyes of a lamb, they could even give God lessons in innocence. I'm so close to these eyes I can feel the beat of eyelashes but I know more about the secrets of the next world than what lies behind them. Eyes where angels might bathe, eyes clear as streams running down snow peaked mountains, eyes that never close, never. Close your eyes, Melisande, or I'll close them myself. Don't put your hand to your throat. And no, don't try to escape. Here. Give me your hands. Your hands are too hot, Melisande, go away, your skin disgusts me. No, I have you by the hair now, let's put this hair to some use at last. Move: left. Right. Left again. Forward. Back. Down, bow down now, down to the ground. Haha. I'm already laughing like an old man.

Arkel Golaud!

Golaud (*suddenly very calm*) Actually, you can do as you please. I couldn't care less. I'm too old for this. And I'm not a spy. I'll wait until chance comes my way and then – but only because it's the custom.

Arkel What's wrong with him? Is he drunk?

Melisande No, but he doesn't love me any more. And I am not happy . . . I am not happy here.

Arkel If I were God, I would feel such pity for the human heart.

SCENE THREE

One of the terraces of the castle. Yniold is trying to lift a stone that is too heavy for him.

Yniold This stone is very heavy. It's heavier than I am. It's heavier than the whole world and my golden ball is stuck between this horrible stone and the rocks. I can't lift this stone, I think it has roots pulling it into the ground.

I hear sheep bleating. They're coming this way. They want to go right, but the shepherd is throwing mud at them to make them go another way. And now they seem lost. They're coming under the terrace, there are so many of them, they've gone so quiet. Shepherd, why aren't the sheep talking any more?

Shepherd (*off*) Because this isn't the way home.

Yniold Where are they going then if they're not going home? How are they going to get to sleep tonight if they can't get home? It's too quiet here, and it's dark. I'm going to find someone to talk to.

SCENE FOUR

The fountain in the park.
  Pelleas comes on.

Pelleas Everything must end. I've been skipping like a child around the snares of destiny. Who woke me up so suddenly? I'll run away shouting with joy and pain like a blind man escaping his burning house. My father is out of danger, I can't deceive myself any longer. She may not come. I ought to go without seeing her. Sometimes I feel as if I hadn't seen her for a hundred years. And I never had the courage, when she looked at me, to look into her look. If I leave without seeing her again, I'll have no more than a few memories, dripping away like water in a muslin pouch.
  I must see down to the bottom of her heart.

Melisande comes on.

Melisande Pelleas!

Pelleas Is that you, Melisande? Don't stay on the edge of the moonlight like that. We have so many things to say . . . come under the shadows of the lime tree.

Melisande I want to stay in the light.

Pelleas We could be seen from the tower windows.

Melisande I want to be seen.

Pelleas Did you manage to get away without anyone knowing?

Melisande Yes. Your brother was asleep.

Pelleas They'll close the gates in an hour. Why were you so late?

Melisande Your brother was having a nightmare.
And then my dress was caught on the nails of the door.
I ran . . .

Pelleas You're breathless, Melisande, like a bird who's been hunted through the forest. Is it for me you're doing all this? And is it your heart I feel beating in my breast, entwined with mine? Come closer.

Melisande We came here a long time ago.

Pelleas Months ago . . . I didn't know then . . . Do you know why I asked you to meet me?

Melisande No.

Pelleas This may be the last time I see you. I'm going away forever.

Melisande Why are you always saying that you're going away?

Pelleas I have to tell you what you know already. Do you know what I'm going to say to you?

Melisande How could I know? I don't know anything.

Pelleas Don't you know why I have to go away?

   He kisses her suddenly.

I love you . . .

Melisande (*in a low voice*) I love you too.

Pelleas What did you say, Melisande, your voice seems to have sailed from the very edge of the world. I almost didn't hear you . . . you love me? Since when?

Melisande Always . . . since I first saw you.

Pelleas I never heard you before, Melisande, it feels like summer rain, falling softly on my heart. You speak so openly, like an angel under interrogation. I can't believe it, why would you love me? You're not lying to make me smile?

Melisande No. I never tell lies. I only lie to your brother.

Pelleas Your voice is like fresh water, bathing my lips . . . falling on my hands . . . give me your hands . . . such small hands . . . and I didn't know you were so beautiful. I had never seen such beauty before I looked at you. I searched for beauty, but I could never find it. Now I have it . . . Where are you, Melisande? I can't hear you breathing.

Melisande It's because I am looking at you . . .

Pelleas Why do you look at me so solemnly? It's so dark under this tree, come into the light or we won't be able to see how happy we are. We have so little time left.

Melisande Let's stay here. I feel closer to you in the darkness.

Pelleas Let me see your eyes. Melisande, you're not thinking about me right now.

Melisande I am thinking only about you.

Pelleas You were looking elsewhere.

Melisande I was seeing you elsewhere.

Pelleas You don't seem happy . . .

Melisande Yes, I am happy, but I'm sad as well.
I always start crying whenever I think about you.

Pelleas So do I . . . I'm close to you, I'm crying from
happiness and yet . . .

He kisses her again.

You're so beautiful, but it's a beauty shadowed by death.

Melisande You too . . .

Pelleas I didn't love you the first time I saw you.

Melisande I didn't either . . . I was frightened.

Pelleas I couldn't look into your eyes, I wanted to go
away immediately.

Melisande I didn't want to come tonight, I don't yet
know why I was so frightened.

Pelleas There are so many things we'll never know, we
wait and we wait . . . and then . . . what's that noise?
They're closing the castle doors.

Melisande Yes.

Pelleas Can you hear that screech of locks? The rumble
of chains. It's too late now . . .

Melisande So much the better.

Pelleas You? Yes. It's what we wanted. We're lost now,
we're saved too. It's no longer about what we want . . .
Come with me. My heart's gone mad, pounding, leaping
through my body, rapture.

He takes her in his arms.

Can you hear it? I'm going to be suffocated by my own
heart. Come into the beauty of the shadows.

Melisande There's someone behind us!

Pelleas I can't see anyone.

Melisande I heard a noise.

Pelleas I hear only your heart beating against the darkness.

Melisande I heard the crackle of dead leaves.

Pelleas It was the wind coming to rest. It dropped when we were kissing.

Melisande Look how far our shadows stretch tonight.

Pelleas They tangle deep down to the bottom garden. Look how far they've gone from us to snatch their kiss. Look.

Melisande (*in a strangled voice*) He's behind a tree!

Pelleas Who?

Melisande Golaud!

Pelleas Where? I can't see anything.

Melisande There. Where our shadows come to an end.

Pelleas I saw him. We mustn't turn around.

Melisande He has his sword with him.

Pelleas I don't have mine.

Melisande He saw us kissing.

Pelleas He doesn't know that we've seen him. Don't move or he'll pounce. He'll stay there as long as he believes we haven't seen him. Go this way. I'll wait for him and stop him.

Melisande I can't.

Pelleas Go quickly. He's seen everything.

Melisande So much the better.

Pelleas He's coming. Give me your mouth, Melisande, your mouth.

Melisande Yes, yes . . .

They kiss, they can't stop.

Pelleas The stars throw down their light . . .

Melisande Covering us . . .

Pelleas More, and more and more. One more.

Melisande Yes, everything, all.

Golaud rushes on them with his sword in his hand and strikes Pelleas who falls by the fountain. Melisande, horrified, flees.

Melisande Why don't I have more courage? Why?

Golaud follows her across the woods, silently.

Act Five

SCENE ONE

The basement rooms of the castle.
Servants. Children can be heard playing outside.

Serving Woman It will be tonight, you'll see. They won't let anyone into the room, you can hear the flies walking on the walls in there. Dear God, it wasn't happiness that came into this house when I opened the doors of the castle.

I'm the one who found them, they were lying in front of the door, like two beggars going hungry, huddled next to each other. She was almost dead, and Golaud still had his sword . . . the doorstep was covered in blood. Even so, he didn't manage to kill himself, he's too big. She, on the other hand, has the slightest of wounds, and yet she is one who is going to die. I ask you, does that make sense? A little wound, under her left breast, a wound that wouldn't even kill a wood-pigeon.

But then, she only gave birth three days ago, she gave birth on her deathbed, there's a sign for you. And what kind of child did she bring into the world? A beggar wouldn't want to own up to such a little waxen figure who's come too soon, who has to be wrapped in lamb's wool, no, it's not happiness that came into this house. And what about the good lord Pelleas? We're not allowed to ask about him, but I know he's at the bottom of the fountain, but they won't talk about it, they won't tell the truth. They're afraid of us, they keep their eyes down and they speak in low voices, you'd think they all conspired together and committed these crimes in unison.

I can't hear the children, they've gone quiet. It's time to go up.

Nobody really knows what they've been doing. What's to be done when the masters are afraid?

SCENE TWO

Rooms in the castle.
  Golaud, the Doctor, Arkel.
  Melisande on a bed.

The Doctor She can't be dying of this tiny little wound, my good Lord Golaud, a bird wouldn't die of it. You mustn't torment yourself so, it isn't you who killed her. It is simply that she could not live. She was born for no reason . . . to die . . . and she is dying for no reason, and we may yet save her.

Arkel Look with what weariness she sleeps, as if her soul had been chilled through.

Golaud I killed without reason. It's enough to make the stones weep. They were only kissing, like little children, they were brother and sister after all. But I couldn't help myself!

The Doctor I believe she is waking up.

Melisande Open the big window so I can see . . .

Arkel Doesn't the air feel too cold for you, Melisande?

The Doctor We must do what she asks.

Melisande Thank you . . . is the sun going down?

Arkel Melisande, how do you feel?

Melisande Very well. Why do you ask? I feel well, but as if I know something, I don't know what I know . . . I'm not saying what I want to say.

50

Arkel You were delirious these past few days, Melisande, and we couldn't understand you at all, but that's all over now.

Melisande Are you alone in the room, Grandfather?

Arkel No, there's the good doctor who has cured you and then there is someone else . . .

Melisande Who is that?

Arkel It is . . . but you mustn't be frightened, he doesn't mean to do you any harm and he'll go away if you're afraid of him, but he's very unhappy.

Melisande Who is it?

Arkel It's your husband, Melisande, it's Golaud.

Melisande Golaud is here? Why doesn't he come closer to me?

Golaud drags himself to the bed.

Is that you, Golaud, I can hardly recognise you, I have the evening sun in my eyes. Why are you turning your face to the wall? You're so thin and you've got much older. Has it been a long time since we've seen each other?

Golaud (*to the others*) Please, would you leave the room for a moment? I'll leave the door wide open, but I must say something to her or I won't be able to die. Please don't deny me this, I'm so unhappy.

Arkel and the Doctor leave.

Melisande, do you feel as much pity in your heart for me as there is in mine for you? Can you forgive me, Melisande?

Melisande Of course I forgive you, what am I to forgive you for?

Golaud I've caused you so much pain, Melisande, I see it all now . . . ever since the first day. It's all my fault, everything that has happened and that will happen is my fault, but I loved you so much! I loved you too much and now someone must die. I am going to die and I want to know, I have to ask you, and you must tell the truth to someone who is about to die, swear to me you'll tell me the truth.

Melisande Yes.

Golaud Did you love Pelleas?

Melisande Of course I loved him. Where is he?

Golaud You don't understand me. You don't want to understand me. What I am asking you is . . . did you love him with a love that is forbidden? Were you guilty? Tell me, were you? Yes?

Melisande We weren't guilty. Why do you ask?

Golaud Melisande, tell me the truth for the love of God!

Melisande Haven't I told the truth?

Golaud Don't tell lies before you die!

Melisande Who is going to die? Am I going to die?

Golaud You and then, after you, I too will die. We must have the truth, tell me everything and I'll forgive you everything.

Melisande Why am I going to die? I didn't know that.

Golaud Now you know and you still have time. The truth! Melisande! The truth!

Melisande The truth . . . the truth . . .

Golaud Where are you now, Melisande? Where are you going?

Arkel and the Doctor stand at the door.

You can come in now. I don't know anything. It's
useless. She's already gone away from us and I'll never
know. I'm going to die here like a blind man chained to
his own darkness.

Arkel What have you done to her? You're going to kill
her!

Golaud I already have killed her.

Melisande Is that you, Grandfather?

Arkel Yes, Melisande, what would you like me to do for
you?

Melisande Is it true winter's here?

Arkel Are you cold, shall we shut the window?

Melisande Not until the sun has sunk to the bottom of
the sea, but it's going down so slowly. I'm frightened of
the cold.

Arkel Would you like to see your child?

Melisande What child?

Arkel You gave birth to a little girl . . .

Melisande Where is she?

Arkel It's here.

Melisande I don't even have the strength to hold her in
my arms.

Arkel You're still very weak, Melisande, I'll hold her
myself so you can look at her.

Melisande She's very small. And she doesn't want to
laugh . . . I feel such pity for her . . .

*The room fills with shadows. Serving women place
themselves along the wall.*

Golaud gets up suddenly.

Golaud What's going on? What are these women doing here?

The Doctor They've come . . .

Golaud Who asked them to?

The Doctor shakes his head.

Golaud What are you doing here? No one called you. Answer me!

No one moves or answers.

Arkel Don't speak so loud, she's closed her eyes, she's going to sleep.

Golaud It's not because –

The Doctor No, look. She's breathing.

Arkel Her eyes are brimming with tears. Now it is her soul that is crying. Why is she holding out her arms like that? What does she want?

The Doctor She's holding out her arms to her child. It's the mother still fighting against death . . .

Golaud Now? You have to say it, tell me!

The Doctor Perhaps . . .

Golaud I have to tell her. Melisande! Leave me alone with her.

Arkel Don't go near her! You don't understand the needs of the soul at this moment.

Golaud She's closing her eyes.

Arkel Speak as softly as you can. We must not worry her. The human soul likes to go away in solitude. She is such a timid little creature, so tentative even in her suffering. Ah, the sadness, Golaud, the sadness of it all . . .

The servants go onto their knees.

What is it?

The Doctor feels Melisande's pulse.

Yes. They're right.

A long silence.

Arkel I saw nothing at all. Are you certain?

The Doctor Yes, I'm certain.

Arkel She left us without a word . . .

Golaud (*sobbing*) Oh –

Arkel Don't stay here any longer, Golaud. Silence is what she will need from now on. Come, it's terrible, but you're not to blame. She was a tiny and fragile being, shy, silent . . . she was mysterious and delicate, as we all are. Look at her, so young, she could be the older sister of her own child. Come. Oh my God, I don't understand any of it either, I never will. Come, the child mustn't stay in this room any longer. It is the child who will have to live in her place, poor little thing, it's her turn now.

They leave in silence.
The end.